THE
Ten Commandments

Edited by MARY ALICE JONES

Cover illustration by MARY MURRAY

Inside illustrations by
DOROTHY GRIDER

RAND McNALLY & CO

Thou shalt have no other gods before me.

EXODUS 20:1-3

God is very great and very good. God loves us.

Men and women and boys and girls who think of God know that they must not put anything else above God in their thoughts. They know that to do what God wants them to do is more important than anything else.

For God is very great and very good. God loves us.

Thou shalt not make unto thee any graven image.

EXODUS 20:4-5

In olden times men and women sometimes made images of wood and stone. They thought these images could help them when they prayed.

But God was working in the world. By and by the people listened as God spoke to them. They learned that only God could hear them and help them when they prayed.

We know that only God can hear us when we pray. We know that God always helps us because he is wise and loving.

Thou shalt not take the name of the Lord thy God in vain.

EXODUS 20:7

The great God, the Creator of the heavens and the earth, is the holy one. Men do not speak of him carelessly. They speak of him reverently. They speak of him lovingly. For God is very great, and God is very good.

The heavens declare his glory, and all the people in the earth stand in awe of him. He makes light to shine out of darkness and tells the number of the stars. He comforts the sad and lonely and is mindful of all his children.

He is God. His name is holy.

Remember

the sabbath day,

to keep it holy.

EXODUS 20:8-10

In the plan of God for man's happiness there is a place for quiet and rest and worship.

To help God's children think of him and talk with him, there is a special day set aside. In the Bible it is called the sabbath. On this day men and women do not go to work. Boys and girls do not go to school. They go to church to sing and pray and think together of God's plan for them and for all men everywhere.

Honor thy father and thy mother.

EXODUS 20:12

In the family mothers and fathers help their children in many, many ways, long before the children can understand about it or can say, "Thank you." As the children grow older, they do many things for their fathers and mothers. Mothers and fathers and boys and girls help one another, not because they must, but because they love one another. Though their parents sometimes make mistakes, boys and girls know that their parents are wiser than they are. They know their parents want what is best for their children. And so they show respect to their parents and trust them and obey them.

Thou shalt not kill.

EXODUS 20:13

God only is great enough to make life. No man can make even the tiniest seed or blade of grass or flying bird. But God, the Creator, gives life to all creatures. "It is he that hath made us, and not we ourselves."

It is God's plan that each one of his children should live happily, without fear that his neighbor will take away his life. It is God's plan that each one of his children should help take care of the life of all his other children. It is God's plan that his children should protect all his creatures. For life is the gift of God. It is sacred.

Thou shalt not commit adultery.

EXODUS 20:14

It is the plan of God that his children live in families. It is his plan that a man and a woman should love one another and make a home together and rear children. The father and mother and children have other friends, whom they like and enjoy. But the members of the family care for one another more than for any other friends. The mother and the father do not love any other man or woman as they love each other.

Fathers and mothers who love one another and love their children are God's best helpers. For they are carrying out God's plan that a man and a woman love each other and rear children. This is God's plan for a happy world.

Thou shalt not steal.

Because God loves all his children, he wants his children to share with one another. If one is hungry or cold, it is God's plan that someone else should help him have clothes and a house to live in and food to eat.

It is right that any man or woman or boy or girl who really needs something should *ask* for it. But it is wrong for any person to *take* what belongs to someone else. That is stealing.

To keep more than one's share when someone else is in need, and to take what is not one's own, both make people unhappy.

Thou shalt not bear false witness against thy neighbor.

EXODUS 20:16

To tell the *good* one knows about someone else may help him. To tell of something bad which the person has done may hurt him. But to say that a person has done something bad which he has not really done is very sure to hurt him. Often it is easy to blame someone else for an accident. Sometimes it is easy, even, to blame someone else for one's own carelessness. And once in a while a boy or girl does something he knows is wrong and when harm comes from it, he says someone else did it. That, God tells us, is a sin.

Thou shalt not covet.

EXODUS 20:17

It is easy to want something which someone else has. But God tells us that it does not make us happy to think about what someone else has and to wish it were ours. It is better to think of the good things we have and to enjoy them and share them with others.

If we really need something more than we have, we may ask God to help us to work and to plan wisely so we may have it. God loves us and knows all the things we need. He helps us get what is good for us.

THE TEN GREAT WORDS

THESE great laws which came to be known as the Ten Great Words, or the Ten Commandments, were very precious to the men of olden times. By and by they came to be written. The people took very good care of them. Often they failed to obey them, but always they came back to them and knew they were *good* laws. And through all the years, from those days to the present time, the Ten Commandments have helped people to know the law of God.

In the Bible there is a wonderful story about this great set of laws. It is the story about how these laws came to be known to the people. The story shows how much the people believed in these laws, how important they thought the laws were. It shows that the people knew the laws were, indeed, the laws of God.

In our Bible these great laws have been kept for us. You can find them and read them for yourself. They are in the book called Exodus, the second book in the Bible. You will find them in the twentieth chapter of this book, that is, in Exodus 20:1–17.

THE STORY OF THE TEN COMMANDMENTS

"SHALL we always be slaves?" the people asked. "Shall we always be hungry?"

It was long, long ago. The people called the Israelites had been living in the land of Egypt for many years. They had built their homes there, they had prospered, and there they had reared their children.

But then there came to the throne in Egypt a king who feared the Israelites lest they become too powerful in his country. And so he passed cruel laws against them. The people lost all their rights and became slaves. They were very unhappy. They wanted to get away from the cruel king.

Now there lived at the court of the king a young Israelite who was the adopted son of the king's daughter. His name was Moses.

Moses saw how cruelly the Israelites were treated. He saw them beaten. He saw them driven with great whips. Moses became very angry. He could no longer live at the court of the king. So he ran away and hid in the desert.

In the long nights under the bright desert stars he thought of his people. He thought of the great God, Jehovah. And one day, in the quiet of the desert, God spoke to Moses.

"I have seen the afflictions of my people in Egypt. And I will deliver my people out of the hand of the Egyptians and bring them to a good land.

"I will send you into Egypt, that you may bring forth my people out of slavery."

Moses was frightened. "Who am I that I should lead forth the people out of Egypt?" he asked.

But the voice of God spoke again. "Certainly I will be with you."

And so Moses went back to Egypt. He told the Israelites what God had promised.

The people listened to Moses. And finally they escaped and made their way into the wilderness. They traveled by day and by night.

The journey was long. The hot sands of the dry country burned the feet of the travelers. But they did not stop. They were on their way to a new country, a land where they could build their homes and live free from slavery.

The people went on and on and on. The way was long. Food and water were scarce. The people became discouraged. They began to grumble.

"This is as bad as being a slave in Egypt," they said. "Moses said God had promised to help us. Has God forgotten his promise?"

Moses heard the grumblings of the people.

"Here at the foot of Mount Sinai let us make camp," he said. "And we will pray to God and he will help us."

So they made camp at the foot of Mount Sinai. And Moses prayed to God, and God comforted him. And Moses comforted the people.

But Moses knew that the people needed something to remind them always of the presence of God and of God's laws.

So Moses went away by himself, up the lonely slopes of Mount Sinai. There he stayed many days and nights. He prayed to God to help him know how God wanted the people to live. And after a while he knew the laws God wanted the people to obey, the laws which would enable them to be happy and to build a good life in the new country.

Then Moses found two smooth stones. And on the stones the laws of God were written.

When he came down from the mountain, Moses called the people together and showed them the tablets on which the laws of God were written. He said to the people, "These are the words which the Lord has commanded, that you should do them." And he read the laws to them.

Then over Mount Sinai bright lightning

flashed through the clouds, and there was a mighty roaring of thunder. The people said, "It is the Lord." And they bowed down and worshiped. And they said to Moses, "All that the Lord has spoken unto us, that we will do."

Then Moses told the people to make an ark, or chest, carefully designed and made of the best wood, overlaid with gold. And Moses put into the ark the tablets of stone on which were written the laws of God.

Special men were named to carry the ark as the people traveled on to the new country.

The years passed. The people had become a nation. In the capital city the king built the most beautiful temple in all the world. And in the temple the central place was given to the ark. For in the ark were the tablets of stone on which the laws of God were recorded.